Market Your Business Online

The Blueprint Book To Grow Any Business Online

Peter Jason Clarke

Market Your Business Online

Please note the information contained within this document is for educational and entertainment purposes only. All effort has been executed to present accurate, up to date, and reliable, complete information. No warranties of any kind are declared or implied. Readers acknowledge that the author is not engaging in the rendering of legal, financial, medical or professional advice. The content within this book has been derived from various sources. Please consult a licensed professional before attempting any techniques outlined in this book.

By reading this document, the reader agrees that under no circumstances is the author responsible for any losses, direct or indirect, which are incurred as a result of the use of information contained within this document, including, but not limited to, — errors, omissions, or inaccuracies.

Table Of Contents

Market Your Business Online

Page 2

Introduction

This book is the first step, and it will help you to start making money on the Internet. Many people have succeeded in this goal, and now you want to do it too.

Maybe you want some extra income from a side business, or perhaps your goal is to build a good living from a business that lets you travel the world. Maybe you already sell your services online, but you want to scale your revenue beyond just charging for more hours. These are all possible by learning how properly to package your skills and knowledge online.

Many people are attracted to the concept of a passive income, that is, an income that flows with little additional maintenance. The results are real, but it does not mean you can become rich without hard work. Instead, this book will teach you how to do the heavy lifting at the beginning, and then transitioning that into a constant automated revenue stream.

You might be an independent professional, a freelancer, a consultant, a coach, a blogger, or someone else with skills and knowledge other people want to learn. Perhaps you have professional skills like stock trading, web design, or computer programming, or maybe you have other interests like sailing, cooking, or yoga. Whatever your passion, you can create authority as an expert in your field and make more money by selling your knowledge online.

Having skills to share is an ideal way to create a better future for yourself. With the right steps, you can make a consistent passive income, or even a comfortable living, but first, you must understand how this system works.

This book provides the blueprint for each step in the process, from researching your first product to marketing yourself on a global level. It explains how to build an online platform, how to create an automated marketing system, and how to scale an online business and sell your knowledge at a premium price as an expert in your field.

This book is based on over a decade of experience in Internet marketing, years of blogging, and extensive research on platform building, social media management, book marketing, online video course development, and running live webinar trainings. The most important lessons are distilled here, saving you hundreds of hours by providing easy steps to follow.

This system revolves around creating strong digital information products. These are made using your knowledge and skills, and are sold and delivered electronically. It may be packaged as an eBook, online video course, or remote training over the Internet. eBooks are the most well-known type of digital information product, and often the most natural starting point for a new business.

Today it is easy to self-publish an eBook, and almost anyone can do it. You simply write about things you know, create an account on Amazon Kindle, and upload the manuscript and cover design. It is rewarding to see your book published on Amazon, but it is also key to building your authority as an industry expert.

You may have also learned how difficult it is to make money selling books these days. It can be a lot worse for non-fiction authors than fiction writers, since the market and sales volumes are much smaller. With millions of books available on Amazon, competition is fierce, even in narrow niches. Most books are invisible at launch, and then slowly sink to the bottom of the sales lists. The prices for eBooks are also ridiculously low, and most sell for just a few dollars or even less.

The key to creating a passive income is to use your eBook as a starting point for a larger marketing effort. By following the advice in this book, you can learn to effectively monetize your skills and sell the same knowledge at a hundred times the price of most eBooks using the same information. You will learn how to repackage your product and sell it in another form at a much higher price.

This book covers sound principles to develop your product, get more website visitors, find more customers, and sell your knowledge and information products at a premium price. This is the blueprint for how to build a real Internet business with a constant and substantial revenue.

This is not snake oil, though there is certainly a lot of that around online. Nothing comes free, and it will take time, work, and perhaps some luck. However, with the right steps, you can create a passive income and successful online business that will generate profits for years to come.

Who Am I

Before we get into the book, let's talk about who you should trust. There are people who write books about topics they have no experience in and they might not teach you how to make money from home. In this book, we teach you about how to make money from home. It is not like any other books on Amazon.

That's not the kind of person who can teach you how to work from home and make money.

You need someone who knows what they are doing and can teach you how to do it. That is me. I know what I am doing and will show you how to do it.

Market Your Business Online

When I was in my twenties, I decided that I didn't want to work for other people anymore. First person in my family to do this. Didn't know how to start a business, but knew that I wanted to work for myself and not someone else.

I had ideas of my own and many things I wanted to accomplish, and I knew that as long as I worked for someone else, my plans would have to stay on hold. So for years, I trudged along and played the office politics. I worked in a job I barely tolerated, and came home too exhausted to pursue my own dreams.

But then one day I woke up. I was working as a sales representative for a window covering manufacturing business, and as part of my job, I traveled the state selling to and servicing retail window covering companies. My lifestyle consisted of staying in cheap hotels, eating a diet of fast food, and being away from friends and family for long stretches of time. I was considered lucky because I had a good salary, a company car, and certain freedoms that many employees don't have. For example, as long as I met my sales quotas, I was able to set my own hours.

But I was miserable.

And then one day, as I was talking to a client about how she got into business, it hit me. If she could do it, so could I.

I started a business that sold window coverings. After that, I started other businesses. I like the challenge and being able to build something from scratch and make it successful.

I also like the idea of working from home. In all the businesses I have built, (some of which I will teach you about in the chapters that follow), working from home has been my number one priority. In the beginning, it was because I couldn't afford an office space or store front. Finally, it made sense for business

But opening and running a successful home-based business takes more than just a good idea and some motivation. In fact, I'd venture to say that it's one of the most misunderstood phenomena's of our time. And if you go about it with the wrong mindset or a lack of knowledge, you can easily end up a statistic. But if you take the time to learn about how to do it the right way, your chances of success are much higher.

I wanted to live a different life than other people. I dreamed big and now I have the perfect life for me. And if you are reading this, then you probably want the same thing too. So let's start!

- You need a mindset that is willing to do what it takes because this business requires persistence and patience.

 - There are many different types of home businesses, so figure out which type suits your interests or skill set best before beginning the process of building your business!

Start Building Your Dreams

When you were young, you probably never thought that someday you would work at someone else's company. Sometimes they will ask for help in their business. You help them live a good life and buy things like a new home or send their kids to college. This is how people get money when they are old and need to retire.

But if you work for someone else, that's exactly what you're doing.

A business wants to make money. The business needs people to work for it. The company makes more money when you work for them, because you do things that no one else can do. Some companies measure how much they make from workers. It is called the 'revenue per employee.' A single person can make a lot of money for a company if they are doing their job well and other people cannot do it as well.

·   An employee at Starbucks earns his company an extra $79,821 each year..

·   A person who works at Google earns the company an extra $1.2 million a year.

The company is making money off of the work that you are doing. They pay you less than what your work is worth.

Isn't it time you worked to build your own dreams?

That's where this book comes in. If you've bought it, I think it's safe to assume you fall into one of these categories:

·   You've been laid off, are in between jobs, or just looking for change and want to do something that will positively affect your financial life.

·   You have a family to care for, and are tired of disappointing them financially.

·   You've always dreamed of owning your own business, but aren't sure where to start.

·   You want to start your own business, but don't have a lot of cash to invest.

·   You're just out of college, and the prospect of entering the corporate rat race makes you want to run and hide.

·   You're a stay at home mom who wants to contribute to the family income, but are hindered because you also want to care for your kids.

·   You're retired and are looking for a new challenge that you can tackle on your own terms.

·   You work for someone else and are tired of building their dreams instead of your own.

If any of the above scenarios describes your circumstances, you might be at the exact place in your life to start a home-based business. Unlike other types of businesses, it's possible to work from home with very little investment and no college training. In fact, the ten business ideas I list in this book can all be started with little to no money, no hardcore training, and you can actually wake up tomorrow morning and begin.

How's that for pursuing your dream?

Ready to start? First, we should talk about what it means to have your own business. It will be hard work but you still can make money. There are some common myths about self-employment that are not true but they sound like they are.

Myths:

*You need to be a college graduate.

*Every business needs an office with employees and equipment.

*A successful business has to have major marketing initiatives, including advertising on TV or in the paper

The reality is that you can start your own home-based business without any of those things – heck, for some businesses like consulting or freelance writing it's actually better if you don't get stuck in one place all day long! And even when there are offices involved (there usually are), they may not require fancy furnishings or expensive leases because the work doesn't take place inside them. Bottom line? If you want to spend more time raising kids, or living abroad, or working from your laptop in a coffee shop – you can do that.

But before we get into the nitty-gritty of all these freelancing topics, let's first talk about what it means to be self-employed and why people go freelance in the first place.

*It might seem like an obvious choice for someone who has always wanted to work on their own terms, but there are plenty of other reasons too! You may want more freedom (and control) over where you live and when you work; you could have lost your job due to downsizing or outsourcing; maybe your company doesn't offer a retirement plan...or any benefits at all. Whatever the reason is, being self-employed is not a bad thing.

 *There are many ways to go about it, too! You could start your own business and be in complete control of all aspects from finding clients (or hiring staff) to setting rates; you can become an independent consultant or work for others as a freelancer while maintaining limited liability protection...there's no one-size-fits-all approach that will work best for everyone.

*In this article we'll talk about the basics: how much does freelance income fluctuate? What types of taxes do I need to worry about? And what should I know before going out there on my own?

What types of taxes do I need to worry about?

There are two different tax situations at play: your income and the business expenses.

The first is easy: you're an independent contractor, so any money from freelancing should be considered taxable income. Income varies with the type of work (there are different rates for jobs like web design or marketing) but it will also depend on what's included in the price. If you provide a service that includes things like lunch or transportation to get to site, then those should be accounted as part-of-the-package costs because they reduce your overall total profits.(If not, then all these extra perks would need to be listed separately.) *

...Should I know before going out there on my own?

The best way to find out what goals make sense for each individual is to start with a plan.

The costs that are involved in starting up a freelance business can be pretty high, so it helps to have savings or money from previous jobs saved in case of emergencies.

...to make the best choice for you and your company, investigate what skills are needed at first (web design? marketing?) then look into how much experience is required before you'll land good work. Once there's enough information on both sides it should become clearer which path will work best for your situation.(However if not found after researching all possible options, whether personal or professional), it could still take time - even months - before one feels confident about their decision-making abilities and knowledge base.

What Others Won't Tell You About Working from Home

Some people sit on the beach and work. They have their laptop and they can earn money. People say that these people are selling something but they don't know what it is.

If that's what you're after, you bought the wrong book.

It's hard to have a successful home business. You need to work really hard. It's probably not true that you can do it without working too.

Many people own a home business. They make up a lot of the economy's money. For example, 52% of small businesses are home-based and those business owners earn combined revenues of $929.6 billion.

That's a lot of successful home-based businesses, and an indication of just how much money there is to be made. But before we begin talking about the specific ways to start your own business, I think it's important to talk frankly with you about some of the most commonly believed misconceptions about working from home so you'll have a realistic expectation of what it will take.

Lie #1: You Only Have to Work When You Want to

This is absolutely true—IF you don't want to be a success. Owning a business is just like anything else you do in your life: the more you put into it, the better your chances of success. And if you go into it with the attitude that you'll only work when you feel like it, you aren't likely to be a success.

According to Inc. Magazine, many small business owners work for 50 hours each week and 25% of them work more than 60 hours per week. This is a lot more than the average employee who works 33.8 hours a week according to the Bureau of Labor Statistics

People are being tricked and lied to by the get rich schemes. These tricks convince people to buy their phony products but they are not true. It takes a lot of work and commitment if you want to build your dream.

Lie #2: You Don't Have to Answer to Anybody

You are the owner of your business and you can only answer to yourself. But you forgot something important: customers.

It doesn't matter what type of business you start, you will have customers. There is always an end user for your products or services, and as a business owner, it's up to you to work around their schedules, make them happy and ensure that they're satisfied so they continue to buy from you. You also want them to tell their friends and families about you, and they won't do that unless you treat them like the boss.

And while it's true that you will make the majority of decisions about how to run the business, you will still have to answer to each and every one of your customers. So, instead of one boss, you'll have dozens. Still with me? Good, let's bust another home business lie.

Lie #3: I can Quit My Day Job Immediately

Many people believe that once you start a home-based company, the business will roll in and before long, you'll be earning a big, fat salary. But the truth is that you will have to build your business slowly and steadily, just like any other business owner does. If you rely on the income from your current job to pay your bills, you should build your business slowly while maintaining your day job so you don't fall short financially.

It's natural to want to jump in feet first and run your new business, but if your finances won't allow it, you simply don't have the option. Many people have begun their home-based business on the side while working their regular jobs, and do so until the business brings in enough profit to substitute for the lost paycheck. Working toward this long term goal will pay off in the long run with a solid, stable business. Plus, if you make a mistake when getting your business off the ground, having another paycheck will allow you to financially recover from it more easily.

Lie #4: I Need a College Education to Start a Business

A study done by the US Census Bureau found that just over half of people who start a business from their home do not have a college degree. That means almost 50% of home-based businesses are started by someone without one.

Some people think this is because business owners tend to be mavericks and want to do things their own way. Other's think it's because once an entrepreneur gets a business idea, they don't want to take the time to get a four year degree when they could be building a business instead. Whatever the reason, I can tell you this. If you choose a business that does not require specific training, like an IT focused business or other area of specialty, you can do well without a college degree. I know this because I don't have one, and I've managed to build several successful businesses.

Lie #5: Clients Won't Take Me Seriously if I Operate My Business from Home

A long time ago, home-based business owners had to hide the fact that they worked from home from their clients. They were forced to rent temporary suites in buildings so clients wouldn't guess they didn't have a commercial location. Luckily, times have changed.

Now that more than half of U.S. businesses are operated out of homes, the attitude has changed, and it's widely accepted to do business with home-based entrepreneurs.

But just because it's accepted, that doesn't mean you don't have to be professional in your dealings with customers. For example, no client wants to hold a business conversation on the phone with a child screaming in the background. And if your business requires in-person meetings with clients, you should section out a portion of your home where they will have the least amount of contact with your living quarters. You might convert a portion of your garage into an office, an attic space, or add an outside door to a spare bedroom.

Even if you don't meet with clients, it will make life easier for you if you dedicate a portion of your home to your business and keep it neat and organized. And if you have small children at home, you'll need to work out a schedule so that when you're at work, they're looked after by someone else.

Okay, now that we've talked about the common myths that surround home-based businesses, let's delve into the ten business ideas I promised you. And remember, in each chapter, I'll give you all the information you need to get started on that business idea—today if you want to!

The Proper Mindset

Market Your Business Online

Okay, I know You want to have like, just quit your job and just gain financial freedom, enough time to spend with your family and your friends or make just enough to go traveling or you want to build, well, I don't know if I could help you build $1 billion business, but there's definitely a lot of million dollar businesses that get made online all the time. You can even start selling your own products as a side-hustle, while you're still working. And then if you are successful, you may be able to turn it into your full-time job.

So whatever it is, set that *intention* and know that just if you work hard enough, you don't give up, I bet you can do that. And this is the best business opportunity to do that right now in history.

You may ask yourself, if it is so easy why so many people fail? Well, you're not gonna fail, but why do people in general, statistically fail? So I'm going to tell you all the roadblocks that stop most sellers and then how you guys can get past it.

You have to see yourself like a bamboo tree. Do you know about bamboo tree? I was completely shocked when I discovered that this amazing plant stays as a seed for five years, yes five years, and all that whole time is just underneath there not doing much, but it's growing roots and all sorts of other stuff, building its foundation for growth.

And then after five years, if it's taken care of that whole time and everything is right, it grows 90 feet in six weeks. Just exponential growth. And that's exactly what will happen to you. But you need to take care of yourself.

So the question is, how long did it take for that tree to grow 90 feet? It took five years in six weeks. Every single bit of that process is what was required for that tree to grow. Okay. And if it didn't, like if you don't take care of that tree for those five years, if you don't take care of you of what you want to do, your plan, your project, your business, well it's not going to grow.

Now, in this part of the book you are going to see the essentials to get started with the whole business, you are going to see what makes a successful product even if you want to go online.

You have to be able to get inside the mind of your potential customer. Remember, especially online, the two things you got is your product and your listing. Online, remember the only thing you got is your listing. They can't touch, feel, taste, your product, none of that. It's all just those photos in those descriptions and, soon or later, reviews. So you got to put all your effort and time into those when you get started.

Your Business Seen Through Digital World Lens

In today's day and age, if you are not advertising on the Internet, you are losing a significant amount of business. It doesn't matter if you are going to be a savvy or not. You must find your way to be online anyway.

You advertise your business in local newspapers, local television and even local radio. That is good. You are getting enough business to keep you afloat. You may receive inquiries from the surrounding cities, or even the bordering states, and that is great.

What if you could attract business from another country?

Market Your Business Online

When you finally decide to take advantage of technology, the Internet is an incredible universe of its own.

When you create a Website, and starting an e-commerce trade, you are opening your business to a whole new world. But nowadays there are different options even though you are not an online expert.

Businesses that would not know that you exist are now able to view your website, research your services and contact you with any questions.

By taking advantage of the Internet, you are allowing your business to grow in ways that it could not if you were to advertise with conventional methods.

In recent years, the e-commerce trades as raised a steady twenty-five every year, and experts feel that this trend will continue. When you finally decide to take the plunge and get your business started on the Internet, there are a few steps that you should take before starting. This will be a nerve wrecking, nail biting point in the growth of your business.

There are steps to take before jumping in. As with any new venture, you need to do some research. Find out what the statistics and trends are for your type of business.

Let me tell you that you are in advantage compared to the other online beginners because at least, you know which direction you are taking, you want to work online!

It is really much easier to manage a store or anything online related to your interests, it cannot be denied.

Attention, I am are not saying that it is not possible to do it inside a niche that you do not know or that does not represent your direct passion, for example if you can't work woods and you are more passionate in creating intangible files, surely it will be a little bit more complicated, because you must the materials and how it reacts to the design.

This is because if you have knowledge of the topic covered in your niche, you will be able to more easily recognize the elements of value to offer to your potential customers. The more specific and specialized you are the more you win over your competitors.

You will be able to identify the best products to market, using qualitative and high-level descriptions.

You will be able to answer even the most technical and complex questions your customers will ask you and it will be much easier to identify all the elements to be used to get a better grip on the public.

Brainstorming Section

As Benjamin Franklin supposedly once said, "If you fail to plan, you are planning to fail."

So, go with this very useful step by step essential guide to start your business and don't quit until you made it.

Phase 1

1. Think and write down your plan of action. There is no path for those who don't have clue where they are going to.

The first things you need to determine are:

-What kind of product you're going to sell,

-What type of customers you're going to reach,

-How you are going to find them.

For example: you want to sell customized woods for little coffee shops or little farms. You don't want to take risk, so it is better to test in your local area to see how it goes.

2. Search about your competitors

What your competitors top-selling products are

How much they charge for their products

What channels (online or offline, or both) your competitors are using for marketing

Find out where your competitors are lacking

You need to take your time and make a marketing research about your competitors success and about their products.

Phase 2

Cost of Materials –

You have to try to only buy as much material as you might need but don't get discouraged because it is never perfectly optimized.

Market Your Business Online

1. Make sure the cost of material is actually at a bare minimum,

-consider also all the activities involved, which includes manifacturing, purchasing, and delivery

-the quality of the material and the final product must be high enough to satisfy the customer need

there is going to be some unused scraps and material when buying in bulk.

Phase 3

Who do you sell to? What should you sell? Where can you sell it?

I know that you are excited to start selling your products, but it is important to take responsible steps before starting.

Many of your business decisions will depend on your target audience, so it is essential to identify your target audience, first.

For example, if you r Business Idea is to create Menu Boards, your possible Target Audience can be restaurants or coffee shops in your city

Phase 4

Testing your Business

You don't want to create a product that nobody wants to buy, or that would be a complete waste of your time, money and resources.

If you want to succeed in your business you need to take responsible steps and you can test the market to see if people will actually want to buy what you plan to sell. So, give some try by producing few prototypes to offer your unique products to some of potential buyer and see how they react.

If You Make People's Lives Easier You Will Succeed

If you have a knack for organization, a customer service driven attitude, and some computer skills, a virtual assistant business might be the right home-based business for you. More and more business people are hiring virtual assistants to help them rather than hiring full-time assistants because it saves them money in the long run. But that doesn't mean you have to charge low rates. The average price paid for a virtual assistant is between $20 and 45 an hour, and if you specialize, you can charge a lot more than that—closer to $100 an hour. Have your attention? Here's the lowdown on starting a virtual assistant business.

- Figure out what you're good at and how to position yourself. If your background is in marketing, for example, focus on that strength so clients know they can trust you with their marketing needs.

- Determine the right price point by looking around online; see what other virtual assistants are charging for similar services or use a pricing calculator. You should charge enough to make a profit after paying expenses like taxes as well as living costs. This means determining an hourly rate or monthly retainer fee—whatever suits your personality best (some people prefer one over the other). Be clear about whether this includes mileage if it's applicable depending on where you live and work from home half of the time versus working full time from home.

What is a Virtual Assistant?

Virtual assistants have taken the place of yesterday's secretaries. They are smart, well-equipped, and fearless business owners who have the ability to provide exactly what their clients need whether that's administrative, creative or technical skills. Some specialize in certain areas such as project management, sales, bookkeeping, or real estate, while others offer general services. They operate remotely, and have the ability to service multiple clients at one time. Here are some of the tasks virtual assistants perform every day:

·   Communicating with clients via phones or emails

·   Manage their client's calendar and set or cancel appointments

·   Prepare and manage and oversee documents

·   Lead generation and prospect management

·   Follow up with new customers

·   Act as a liaison between the client and his employees

·   Make travel arrangements

·   Prepare spreadsheets, PowerPoint presentations, charts, and slide shows for meetings

·   Data entry

·   Conduct research for projects

·   Create customized solutions to store that research

·   Set up an email autoresponder

·   Database creation

· Transcribing

· Set up social media accounts and/or blog, and then update and manage them

· Answer support tickets

· Event planning

· Direct marketing

These are just a few of the duties successful virtual assistants perform. Basically, you can use any computer skill you have and offer it to busy business people. Are you expert at commenting on blog posts for promotional purposes? Someone needs that. Do you do light bookkeeping? Someone will pay you for that. Are you a trouble shooter and have a knack for building good relationships with people over the phone? Business people hire good customer service reps all the time.

As you can see, a virtual assistant business is good for people who have a lot of skills and want to use them in a business. If this sounds like something that might be right for you, read on to learn more about what it takes.

How Much Money Will it Cost?

Market Your Business Online

You may already have everything you need to start a home-based virtual assistant business. Your main expenses will be related to computer equipment. You will need a computer, printer, internet connection, and software for the services you're providing. For instance, if you plan to offer light bookkeeping, you'll need bookkeeping software. In the same vein, you'll need PowerPoint if you plan to do presentations, Excel for spreadsheets, and word processing software to create documents. So, depending on what you already have, you could start the business for the price of a software package, or if you don't already have a computer, it may cost upwards of $2,000.

You should also have a website, but it's possible to set it up for free by using WordPress or Weebly. Here's a ###a href="https://www.siteground.com/tutorials/wordpress/" rel="noopener noreferrer" target="_blank">free tutorial that walks you through the process of setting up a WordPress site (It includes free videos if you're more of a visual person), and here's a great guide to setting up a Weebly website. (And here's a 42 minute video in case you want visuals for this one, too.)

Tasks:

-Get a domain name and hosting for your website (this is the most expensive part of starting a business, but it's necessary)

-Decide what you want to blog about. It's not required that you write every day - so if you're more creative or analytical by nature, pick

How Much Money Will I Make?

You can make as much money as you want with your work. If you set up your business well, have the right skills, and work hard, you can make a lot of money. According to Payscale, the medium virtual assistant's income is about $65,000. That's the average, so it's important to note that some assistants make less and some make more. There are three ways that virtual assistants typically bills their clients. They are:

· Hourly.Virtual assistants bill their clients by the hour. First, you have to set your rates. These rates can vary depending on the job.For instance, you would charge more for specialized work rather than generalized. If you offer general services, your hourly rates will probably fall between $25 -$40 an hour.

·   Project Fees. Some virtual assistants offer packages to help sell their services. For example, if someone contacts you to handle a direct marketing campaign, rather than charging by the hour, you can quote a fee for the entire project, start to finish. This is also a great way to convince someone to try your services, and hopefully it will turn into a long term business relationship after the first project is completed.

·   Retainer Fees. When you charge a retainer fee, people pay up front so they have your service. For instance, if a client needs you to complete a variety of tasks on a monthly basis that you estimate will take 10 hours, you can give them a slight discount in exchange for hiring you on a retainer basis. A retainer means you are guaranteed the work each month. This would provide the client with a discount and allow you to count on that retainer income month after month.

Money is important. You need to decide how you will get money for your work. You can agree to accept wire transfers directly into your bank account, checks via the mail, or you can utilize an online payment service like PayPal. (You can set up an account for free with just an email address.)

How To Find Clients

If you want to start this kind of business, there are plenty of clients. It seems that virtual assistants are popular in every industry, so the work is abundant. In order to find your first clients, you will have to promote yourself where people are looking. Here are some ideas to do that:

·   Your website. Make sure your website is SEO optimized (Here's a great beginner's guide to help you do that)

·   Online marketplaces. There are many websites that have people who need help with their jobs. These sites allow you to set up a profile and tell potential clients what you have to offer. Before you set up your own profile, check out the profiles of the success virtual assistants already on the site to get an idea of how you should structure yours. Some of the sites you should be on are VirtualAssistants.com, UpWork, Guru, iFreelance, and VA4U.

· In person networking is good. You can meet people in your area and talk about your services. Attend local gatherings of business people, ask friends or acquaintances for referrals, and use your social media accounts to network and talk about your services.

What Tools Will Help My Virtual Assistant For My Business?

Every business needs some tools that will help them do their job. This will help them provide better service to customers. I've put together a list of the tools every virtual assistant needs, many of which are free. I've listed them in categories and provided links to each of the tools so you can find them easily.

Communication Tools

These tools will help you communicate with your clients more easily.

· Skype. You can download the program for free and communicate with your clients face to face, even though you may be hundreds of miles away.

· Mailchimp. You can use this well-known email marketing service for free as long as your mailing list has less than 2,000 people.

·   RingCentral. This handy cloud phone system allows you to plug your desk phone or PC into your internet connection for voice, fax, text or audio conferencing and online meetings with your clients. The service starts at $25 a month, but you can get a free 30-day trail.

Productivity Tools

These tools will allow you to make better use of your and your client's time.

·   My Hours. A free time tracking application for your projects and tasks. For a fee of $2 per additional user, you can add your clients to the project and use it interactively.

·   PayPal. Allows you to bill clients and receive payment online. It's easy to transfer the money to your bank once payment is received.

·   Wave. Free business accounting software. This software also offers free invoicing.

·   Hootsuite. Sign up for free and use this site to manage your social media accounts. You can keep track of connections and schedule posts on all your networks.

· Google Docs. Create and share documents with your clients for free.

· VA Networking.com. You can join this forum for free and interact with other virtual assistants to get questions answered and network with fellow VA's.

Most experts agree that the virtual assistant industry to will continue to grow as executives and other business owners look to online assistance rather than in-office help. If you have computer skills and an ability to work closely with people, this may be a great business for you. It takes little to no money to start, depending on what you already have, and you can set up shop in a day.

But if you don't have the skills needed to operate a virtual assistant business, there are other options for making money online. In the next chapter, we'll take a look at how you can successfully set up and run your own online shop.

Find your niche and focus

Market Your Business Online

One of your most important considerations before you do anything is to define your niche and focus. You may think that your knowledge or services are generic and apply to a large audience. This may well be so, but that line of thinking will not serve you well if you want to create a successful online business.

The problem is that the Internet is crowded these days. There are thousands of lawyers, financial advisors, life coaches, software developers, photographers, yoga instructors, and [fill in your industry or niche] with good visibility online already.

Unless you are in a very specialized niche, you are likely to face stiff competition from competitors who are already well-known to your audience. And so, even though your skills and services may well be useful for a large audience, the trick to building visibility on the Internet is to limit your focus to a much smaller niche where you can stand out from the crowd. In other terms, it is better to be a big fish in a small pond. This is called to 'niche-down'.

By focusing on a more specialized niche, you will also have to accept that you will not target a more general audience that could benefit from your skills and services. The key is to focus, focus, focus.

Pick a niche as specific as possible, but not narrower than there is a market big enough to monetize. You will have to give this a lot of thought. Try to find the intersection of your passions and skills, and a profitable niche specific enough to differentiate from the larger and more generic markets with tougher competition. It is important to niche-down enough, particularly before you have a healthy volume of traffic visiting your website.

For example, you may be a software programmer developing iPhone apps. While you can sell books and other information products on this topic, it might be easier to succeed if you narrow down further, for example to iPhone 3D game development. Thus, you have a better chance of becoming visible, to create authority, and to be perceived as an expert by a larger audience.

Once you have found a unique position in a narrow niche where your skills or services fit the potential customers, you need to be able to sell something. To many, asking for the sale is a scary and difficult moment. In theory, it is actually quite simple.

Since you will rarely be able to sell a product the potential customer does not want to buy or have any use for, it isn't worth trying. You will fail almost every time.

Instead, focus on potential customers who already want or need your product. That way, it becomes easier to get the sale. Try to make the potential customer understand that the hard decision is not to make the purchase, but that without the purchase, their life will be more difficult. This is much easier if you focus on a narrow and specialized niche.

Create your home on the Internet

In the previous section, you learned to find a narrow and well-defined niche in which your skills and services fit the audience perfectly. The more specific your target, the more successful you will be—to a point. After all, your niche must be big enough to contain a sufficient number of people prepared to pay for your products. Later we will discuss what those products might be.

For now, we need to create the foundation of your online business. You need to have a home on the Internet, to which your audience and potential customers will come and find out more about your expertise, products, and services.

To most people, the natural answer is to set up a website. This is certainly true, but a surprisingly large number of people use a Facebook page instead of a website. Why? Because it is so much easier. However, this is a very bad decision.

Your online platform is the basis of everything you do on the Internet, and if you run it only through Facebook, then it is not truly your own. Social media platforms come and go, they change their services or policies, or they may suddenly block your page or do something else that harms your ability to serve your customers. The other consideration is aesthetic and function. While social media platforms are becoming increasing sophisticated, you are still limited to their design restrictions and the function of their tool.

For this reason, you should not rely on a Facebook page as the foundation for your Internet presence. You need to build your own platform by having a website.

Luckily, creating your own website has never been easier. Here is how to create one:

· Find and buy a domain name (such as www.monetizeknowledge.com) that is free and relates to yourself, your niche, or your business.

· Chose a content management system with which to build your website. There are many such systems available, but I strongly recommend WordPress, as it is easy to use, has a large ecosystem of plugins and themes, and is an industry standard. You need to have very specific needs to justify choosing something else.

· Rent a hosted website service that uses the content management system of your choice (such as WordPress). Many hosting suppliers exist, and can be found by doing a web search for 'WordPress hosting'.

·   To personalize and improve the look and feel of your website, download a paid or free theme. A theme is a set of colors and designs that modify the look of your website. Tens of thousands of different themes exist for WordPress, making it easy to change the look and feel to anything you can imagine. WordPress themes can be found in many places, including through the website software itself.

·   Configure the theme after it's installed, for example, by setting your logo and desired fonts and colors.

·   Build your website by adding pages, menus, sidebars, and more. Many WordPress themes come with sample pages you can use and edit.

One of the most important sections to add to your site is the blog. A blog is a free-flowing stream of informal articles on anything that relates to the topic of your niche or industry. You should add blog articles for years to come, preferably weekly. Blog articles should be educational or otherwise share genuinely useful or valuable information.

Blog articles serve several important purposes:

·   They create a natural place for search engines like Google to find and drive traffic to. Thus, blog articles are great traffic generators.

·   A continuous stream of educational and valuable content creates a reason for your website visitors to come back regularly.

·   As blog articles should share knowledge, thoughts, or otherwise be educational or informative, they help build trust and authority.

·   Blog articles are a great place to promote lead magnets (we'll cover this a little later) or products, thus helping to push website visitors through the marketing funnel and closer to the sale.

By now, you should have the basics in place. You have chosen a narrow and well-defined niche with specific needs you can serve well, and you have built a home on the Internet as the foundation for all other Internet marketing and business activities, which will be discussed in the coming sections.

Building an email list

With a website and blog in place, you need to start building your email list (also known as the leads database, or just "list"). What is an email list, and why do you need one?

Having an anonymous website visitor is great, but getting their contact information is much better. That way, you can keep in contact with them, nurture their interest and build trust, and promote offers for your products. Even if they don't come back to your website.

But how do you get website visitors to give you their contact information? These days, offering a newsletter email is not enough to entice your audience.

The trick is to set up a leads generation system using a leads magnet. To harvest email addresses from your website, you should:

·   Create a free leads magnet—digital content your website visitors want to get. This can be, for example, a simple eBook, a short course delivered as emails, a video tutorial, a report, or something else you can offer for free that your audience is eager to get.

·   Create a landing page (a web page) that explains the benefits of the offer and delivers the lead magnet using automated emails after website visitors submit their contact information in a registration form on the landing page.

·   Add highly visible call-to-action buttons that promote the free lead magnet on all your web pages and blog articles. The buttons should have a strong signal color, actionable text like "Get your FREE eBook on [SUBJECT] now", and redirect the visitor to the landing page offering the leads magnet.

With these three steps in place, you have an automated leads generation system that starts to collect email addresses. Please note the sequence above is the order you use when you build the system. The website visitors, on the other hand, experience the process in reverse order. They will:

·   Visit one of your web pages or blog articles, or see an advertisement you run on Facebook, etc.

·   Click a call-to-action button or hypertext link offering something they want for free, such as an eBook PDF (your leads magnet). The call-to-action button redirects the website visitor to the landing page.

·   Read more on the benefits of the offer on the landing page.

·   Submit their contact information in the registration form on the landing page.

·   Get the free leads magnet using an automated email.

The leads magnet you use should be educational or informative, and be perceived as valuable enough to entice website users to register their contact information to get it.

Make sure the leads magnet (your eBook, email course, report, video tutorial, etc.) is truly educational and builds trust. Only promote your products or services in an offhand manner inside the lead magnet; this is not the place for a hard sales pitch. Only show your expertise and build trust at this point.

Provided you have traffic coming to your website (more on that soon), you now have a working system that collects the contact information of your website visitors, thus automatically building your email list.

Growing your email list is one of your top priorities if you want to build an online business and monetize your subject-matter expertise. You can even add several parallel leads generation systems on your website, for instance having multiple leads magnets with related sets of landing pages and call-to-action buttons.

In fact, this is strongly advised, as you can then create different lead magnet offers with distinct targets, which increases the chance one of them will entice a particular visitor to register their contact information.

Sending emails

With a website and a leads generation system in place (lead magnets, landing pages, and registration forms), you should have the basis for a growing email list.

Utilize this email list to keep in contact with your audience and increase their interest and trust. When the time is right, offer your products or services. In short, you can send emails that help build your authority and to promote your products.

Before sending emails on a larger scale, you need to consider four important topics:

·   Deliverability rate and spam filters (how many of the emails arrive to the visitor's inbox)

·   Open rates (how many of those are opened and read)

·   Click-through rates (how many readers actually click on the links supplied in the email)

·   Spam flagging and unregister rates (how many readers are unhappy to get your emails)

All emails you send need to be delivered, opened, and have a click-through to achieve the goal of making the lead engage with you in some way. Crucially, it should not cause the recipient to unregister or flag the email as spam. Knowing how to get your emails delivered, opened, and clicked is a big subject of its own, and is outside the scope of this book. Read my book "Mastering Online Marketing" for full details.

Use your email list for a slow and steady delivery of engaging content (drip delivery). You should not send more than one or two emails per week, or your recipients will likely become annoyed and decide to unregister.

Make sure the majority of your emails provide educational or informative content that benefits the reader (not you), such as your weekly tips on your niche or ways to learn a specific skill. If most of your emails are about you or your products, you will lose much of your following.

Effective examples of emails include:

- Drip delivery of training content

- Weekly or monthly tips & tricks

·   How-to articles

·   Weekly roundup of your latest blog posts

·   Invitations to free webinars

·   Information on new content, like new video tutorials or eBooks

Rarely send emails that promote your products strongly, and save that for product launches, discount offers, or other events. It is perfectly fine to promote your products in the educational emails too, but this needs to be done in an offhand manner with a soft sales message.

The goal is to come across as an expert who is sharing valuable knowledge, not as a salesperson. That will serve you better in the long term by building trust and growing your position as an authority on the topic.

Get traffic to your website

Market Your Business Online

Now that you have found a well-focused niche that fits your skills, have created a website with a leads generation system, and are building an email list that you nurture by sending emails over time, you have a working skeleton for your online business.

The next step is to get traffic to your website. This is by far the most difficult part, and the one that may take the longest time, unless you want to pay for traffic. You choose to attract visitors either by paid advertisements, or for free by offering high quality content.

You can get traffic by investing in paid advertisements such as:

·   Social media advertisements (for example Facebook or LinkedIn ads). Your paid advert is shown in the social media flow of people that fit a particular geographical or demographical filter, or people the social media platform think are interested in certain keywords that relate to your niche.

·   Search engine marketing (like Google AdWords) is when your paid ads are shown in search engine results when someone searches for a particular keyword phrase. The ads shown above, below, and to the right of the search results on Google are the best example.

·   Banner ads on other websites, such as local or niche magazines, web portals, or forums. While search engine and social media ads are easy to set up using a credit card, banner ads on other websites may take some more time to research and deploy.

·   Banner ads or promoted articles in weekly newsletter mailshots some industry magazines send out to their subscribers.

Paid traffic generation produces traffic instantly, but the return on investment depends on how well your website and lead magnet offers attract the visitors to register on your email list, and later to buy your product.

It is also possible to get traffic for free, although it takes longer to see results. To get free traffic, you can:

· Create a big website with many pages and an active blog with many articles that search engines like Google can find and drive traffic to. Be aware that your pages and articles need to have a reasonably large amount of text that relates to the particular search keywords you want to get traffic to—search engines cannot find pages dominated by images but have no text with relevant keywords. This strategy works but is less effective than it used to be due to the massive number of web pages that exist about every conceivable topic, many of which overlap your own content. The trick here is to focus on a well-defined and narrow niche.

· Inbound links from other websites. One of the best ways to get traffic, as well as coming closer to the top of search engine result lists, is to have other websites link to your web pages and blog articles. Try to get as many inbound links as possible. You can get this organically if you have great content, but you can also speed up the process by contacting other relevant blogs and forums. Ask them to review your product, offer to write a guest blog article for them, or respond to forum entries and link back to your own site.

· Social media sharing is another option to get free traffic. Take part in social media groups, share content, offer free leads magnets, and ask your social media friends to share some of your posts and offers. Make sure your social media posts are educational and informative, and do not try to push your message by using spam. A great idea is to promote all your new blog posts on social media. Don't forget to link back to content on your website from your posts. As social media posts may have a short life-span (particularly on the fast-moving Twitter), it may become time-consuming to constantly push out new messages. Social media marketers use robots (like Edgar or Hootsuite) that automate this process, and you might want to do the same.

·   Produce multimedia and publish it on various platforms. For example, you can publish video tutorials on YouTube, publish PowerPoint presentations on SlideShare, publish a podcast on Apple iTunes or SoundCloud, or other media platforms that fit your content. A great option is to write one or more short eBooks and publish them permanently for free on Amazon. Make sure the content you publish on all channels ends with information on a free lead magnet on your website, thus enticing the reader or viewer to visit your website and register for the lead magnet. Make the lead magnet offer a clickable link if the content sharing platform supports that.

Getting traffic organically is a slower process that requires a bigger effort than paying for traffic. However, your content continues to provide marketing value for years to come with no further work or spending on your part, while paid adverts lose their value as soon as the budget is spent. There is no reason you can't do both, of course.

Create and sell products

Market Your Business Online

By now, you have created the skeleton for an online business where you can monetize your subject-matter expertise. You have found a narrow niche in which you can build visibility and become known as a trusted expert. You have a website and blog, and a growing email list with an audience you can nurture through targeted emails. You have also learned how to get traffic to your website using paid and free options.

The final step in creating an online business is to create and sell products you actually make money from. If you have physical products you want to sell, set up a web shop as part of your website. However, this is not a viable option if you want to sell your actual knowledge, rather than physical products related to the same field. Ideally, you will use a low- or no-touch automated digital delivery system to create an (almost) passive income. For this, a different strategy is needed.

The website and free lead magnets discussed earlier were used to get traffic and leads, as well as to build trust and authority. You should now be perceived as an expert, and your audience should be eager to buy your products. What digital information products can you offer if you want to make money from your expertise?

Market Your Business Online

Here are some examples:

- eBooks

- Audio courses

- Video courses

- Consultations

- Private or group training sessions

- Private or group coaching and mentoring

- Consulting services

You should offer products in various price ranges, as it is easier to buy an expensive product from someone you have already purchased a low-cost product from. Few people will buy your most expensive product right away.

Most of your customers will buy the low-cost product, and if you over-deliver, many of them will upgrade to the next-level product. For each step, try to leave the customer desire more, which is fulfilled by the next product that goes into additional detail.

·   Start the sales funnel with a relatively cheap low-end product that most people can buy, for example an eBook or a short video tutorial, that costs about the same as a lunch or dinner (less than $100). This product is preferably auto-delivered using email after the credit card payment has been fulfilled.

·   The next product could be a one to ten hours pre-recorded video training course that teaches your audience how to solve the main problem in your niche. This product should be in the range of $100 to $1,000, depending on the value the knowledge you share has to your customers. Some courses sell for thousands of dollars, depending on the topic and niche. It all comes down to the course's value to the student.

·   For customers who want more, you can offer live group or private training courses that you run online as webinar meetings. Depending on the value of the skills you share and how long the training program is, you can charge anything from $200 to $5,000 for it.

·   If your expertise covers a big or complicated area and your audience can use their new skills to make money in their business or work, you can also offer a long-term coaching or mentoring program that stretches over several months. This could cost $10,000 or more in some niches, if you are a true expert in the field.

You can create an unlimited number of other products, but the concept of selling your books, video or audio training courses, and live training sessions is a common concept that works well for many with skills to share.

The key is that each of these information products cover essentially the same knowledge you would share in a low-cost non-fiction book on Amazon, but repackaged and sold at a much higher price.

The content on your website, free lead magnets, and low-cost products should only teach your audience WHY and WHAT they should do to solve a particular problem. Only the higher-priced products teach your customers HOW to do it, or DO it for them.

That way, you create a path on which your customers start by buying a low-cost product that build trust and reduces the barrier to spending more money on you as a product supplier. As the low-cost product only explains the WHY and WHAT, but not the HOW, he or she is kept wanting more, and is warmed up to a sales offer for your more expensive product once the first product is consumed.

Every product in the price ladder should promote the next product, and to a lesser extent, the one after that, to entice the customers to move forward as soon as they have consumed the previous product. In effect, you create a sales funnel in which some of your customers are eager to buy increasingly more expensive products from you.

Of course, for each new step in the price ladder, fewer people will buy. However, the ones who do are likely loyal, and at the top of the price pyramid, you have customers who love what you offer them and who are prepared to pay a lot for your skills and expertise.

You can also experiment with monthly subscription plans if you have digital products to support that. Subscription models generally help to create a more sustainable income stream than one-off sales, for which you need to re-start the sales funnel each month. Membership sites are a popular route for this.

If you want to create a lifestyle of freedom and run your business using a laptop from anywhere in the world (known as the laptop lifestyle, or being a digital nomad), you should strive to create products that are scalable (auto-delivered eBooks or video trainings) and do not require hours-for-dollars work (such as a one-to-one live training session).

Additional revenue streams may be to sell advertisements on your website or affiliate marketing. The advertisement market requires high traffic volumes to provide any meaningful income, and has the disadvantage that your website is cluttered with content that may be distracting or that you do not approve of. Affiliate marketing is a better idea if you run an expert blog and write non-fiction books.

With affiliate marketing, you mention or recommend other companies' products in your content (in your eBooks, blog articles, video courses, etc.) with a clickable hypertext link. If your readers follow the link and purchase the product, you are attributed to the sale and get a commission. However, many countries now have laws requiring you tell your readers if you are an affiliate receiving money from the recommendation.

The final option is the most difficult one, but it has the potential to transform your one-person expert business into a real company of almost any size. This is to create software products that solve a particular problem for the audience in your niche.

In its simpler form, it can be a smartphone or a tablet app, although that might not be the best choice for a sustainable long-term software business. The better option is to create a web application (known as Software as a Service, or SaaS), for which you charge a monthly or yearly recurring fee for using the functionality hosted on the application service you offer.

Examples of authors and bloggers who created successful software businesses this way include ConvertKit (a smaller business offering email marketing) and HubSpot (arguably the world's leading and most powerful marketing automation system).

Creating software products is expensive and difficult, but can have a large potential. It is best to wait with this until you already have a thriving business using other types of digital information products, unless you happen to have a fantastic idea and a lot of money to invest.

How to approach the E-commerce world with your Business

Here, I want to give to you some essential guidelines that will help you surely to approach the online market at the best, and for any step or strategy that you decide to take or to apply, these fundamentals will let you start, take further steps, and keep going with the best result ever at any stage that you will be going through.

So, here we are, and in the world of e-commerce, I want you to remember these 4 keys, these 4 keys are fundamental to succeed in the e-commerce:

- Flexibility
- Ease of use
- Scalability
- Security
- Flexibility

Researches show that offering gifts and well placed impulse items produce a better marketing approach. This requires an e-commerce solution to be flexible enough to allow various give-aways, coupons and promotions. Also, if your product comes in a variety of models or styles, with different options and different prices then you must communicate these factors and portray them distinctively in your online store. A true business person will certainly follow the patterns of his or her usual clients as well as those who directly visit the site. Web statistic tracking tools can be a great help to this end.

Ease of Use

Some e-commerce stores are very easy to use and require only a few minutes to learn while others are more complex with so many features that they can be overwhelming. Being able to see a demonstration of software before buying it is a great help to determining ease of use.

Scalability

Being able to grow with your company is very important. If you choose a very simple solution now, then require a more robust solution down the road, you will lose time converting your store. If the URL structure of your store is not consistent, you can also lose search engine rankings by changing e commerce solutions. Therefore, it is important to choose an e-commerce solution that can grow with you. For example, some stores owners may not want coupons in the beginning but then down the road decide it is a good idea. Some stores may also have limits on number of products, inventory control and tracking that down the road will be very important.

Security

Of utmost importance to online stores is transaction security. The priority for any business firm should be secure transactions. Thanks to Netscape for introducing SSL (secure socket layer), data can be protected by online store owners. SSL is an encryption technology that encrypts a message and the receiver decrypts it by using RSA security. To enable SSL on your web server you need a digital ID (a form of identification that will recognize you). Many web hosts provide SSL installation for anywhere from a few bucks to a few hundred bucks per year.

Overall, you want flexibility, ease of use, security and scalability in your online store. I recommend you to research your options before you make a final choice, and whenever possible, get a free trial of your solution before you buy.

The Social Media

The Social media is also crucial in the development of this type of business. If you are able to effectively promote your products, you can achieve important performances.

If you are a beginner, aiming for a continuous publication on Instagram and Facebook is already a good start, but if you want to really sell you must go for Etsy and develop your own business online with your own website.

Whilst to manage with success social media it is very important to be consistent in your publications trying to involve your users with "Call to action", or posts that invite surfers to interact with your page.Example: "Tag a friend you might like ...". By creating your own website, selling on Etsy and pinning on Pinterest will not surely make you busy at same way, unless you are selling very much, of course.

In case you are keen of managing the social media, keep in mind that the Call to Action(s) allow to improve the engagement of your users letting you build a real rotating community in your store, and who knows..., in the future to create a real brand.

For social publishing you can think of relying on the Social Rabbit plug-in which will allow you to automate your social posts allowing you to save a significant amount of time.

Choosing the Right Domain Name

Domain names are to websites as book covers are to novels. If they are not interesting enough, or don't properly convey what a website is about, visitor will have no desire to enter them in their browsers. Yet, excessive creativity doesn't make for a good domain name either. Why is this so? It's because if a domain name is creative but not keyword-rich, search engine bots won't be able to index it in search engine listings. So, ultimately, your domain name must be both catchy yet search engine optimized. This article will explain how you can achieve both objectives.

First and foremost you will need to find a popular search engine keyword that can be incorporated into your domain name. A keyword analyzer can help you in this task. These can be found pretty easily with a basic search engine query. When you find one, enter in a keyword that best summarizes the purpose of your website. The keyword analyzer will return different versions of this keyword. If the more specific instances can also fit within the nature of your website, choose one. This is because when it comes to search engine optimization, more specific keywords are better since they are less likely to be used by other webmasters.

Now you can start selecting your actual domain name. Most domain name companies will allow you to see whether or not your domain name is available. If it is not available, it will return a list of recommended domain names. Take advantage of this tool by first entering your selected keyword. If your keyword as a domain name is not available, consider the suggestions the domain name company gives. If the main keyword is still included in these suggestions and it ends with .com, consider it. Otherwise, you will have to be more creative.

For example, you can use 'filler' words, numbers or phrases within your domain name to still include your selected keyword. Fillers could be 'a,' 'an' or 'the.' Search engines tend to not look at these words, so you still have a good shot at getting indexed while having a domain name that is memorable and catchy. You can also consider fillers at the end of a phrase, such as '101'.

What if you do these things and you still can't get .com? Well, there are some situations where it is better to stick with a lesser-used extension because the keyword is just that popular. Extensions that still get noticed include .net, .biz and .org. Additionally, you can also consider using country or state-based extensions if you don't mind international or local-based marketing. It's better to be number 1 in France's version of Google than to be number 200 or worse in America's version of Google.

In conclusion, choosing a domain name that will get the right buzz from both humans and search engines doesn't have to be hard. The keyword analyzer will help you with 90% of your domain name, while your wit with fillers can help you the other 10%. And, if after an immense amount of pondering, you still can't get the .com, you can opt for other extensions.

Choosing the right products to sell

Market Your Business Online

When you first start your online business, the first and most obvious question you will ask yourself is...what am I going to sell? There are several things that you can sell, you can find loads of videos and ideas about it inline. But you can also sell your ideas. If you are a graphic designer or you are really good at creating files that work with software, as long as they are your own design and they are not copyright infringement you can sell your own designs. People are always looking for people who make good designs, not everybody is design savvy and a lot of people just want to be able to make beyond this initial phase of designing.

So there are many questions you have to ask yourself to set your business.

Points to consider when deciding the answer to that question are:

· Is it a tangible item I want to sell?

· Is it light and easy to ship?

· Is it a digital good that is downloaded?

· Is it perishable or fragile?

· Is there enough demand to make your venture profitable?

· Does it have little competition from large online companies (niche products)?

The last characteristic is the one that can be hard to pin down or else it can be your point of advantage, because crafts products win it all in my opinion, always.

Here is a generally accepted method of arriving at an idea of how heavy the demand and competition is for a product.

If you have a special interest in some products that meet the above criteria, great, but don't limit your investigation just to items you like. You are looking for a niche product with relatively good demand (enough to make it profitable), but without heavy competition.

One way to see what the demand is for products you are interested in is to look at search engines to see how frequently people search for the product you are considering.

The result of all this research should be that one or more products will fit into a niche market - products with some demand, and relatively little supply. For the best results, focus on one niche product category, and offer a wide selection. That way, you can become the best online source for that particular category. For example, instead of offering general craft supplies, offer the widest possible selection of needlepoint kits. This strategy will also allow you to rank higher in search engines because you can optimize your pages for fewer, more specific, keywords.

Quality, technical characteristics, specifications, prices, all factors to consider when choosing the products to import into your e-commerce.

Carefully analyze all these factors using one of the most powerful tools to carry out this type of evaluation or customer feedback.

The reviews can actually provide you with even more precise indications of the descriptions offered by the suppliers regarding the quality of the products.

It might also be useful to buy yourself a couple of products to actually understand if the items offered by a particular supplier are actually qualitative.

Once identified, you can proceed with their import in your store.

<u>Pay attention to the size.</u> If it is a tangible item, what you want is selling a creation that is handy and easy to ship. Nothing too big or dangerous. You need to avoid everything to delay the time of the shipment or to compromise it. The general rule is that a good product should be able to fit inside a shoebox and weigh less than 2kg (4.4lb), the weight limit for ###a href="https://www.salehoo.com/blog/what-is-epacket-shipping" rel="noopener noreferrer" target="_blank">ePacket. This is to save you paying extra for shipping. Stick with it!

<u>It is better to create items that are in demand all year round</u>. This is an ideal of the product you will decide but still it is not a must. In fact, selecting a product that you would sell typically for one season a year it is not a big deal because you won't sell during the rest of the year.

If you want to sell well I would recommend to choose products of a price range between 13$ and 220$. If the price is too low you're not going to be making much of a profit margin. And going over 220$ a so high price will discourage people buying.

So, once you have decided about your niche, and please try to choose a niche that is not already done and overplayed, I would try to come up with something different and sell it on Etsy and pin the Pinterest. You can also sell things on eBay, Facebook groups, but in this case I recommend going on your local area groups or in handmade themed groups. Last but not least, take good picture!

###u

If you think that the affiliation is the most suitable option for you, that one is a good idea too. If you are an online passionate, or you are a blogger, or you have an online presence and want to share deals, make your own tutorials for them or you have a quite big following on the internet you can become an affiliate. You can create an affiliate link and if anyone wants to buy a product they can buy it through your link and you will make a little bit of money. This affiliation program is accessible from anyone though.

Grow your business

Market Your Business Online

By now, you know how to create a marketing platform, build an online business, and set up a sales funnel with which you offer products at different price ranges. This is more than just a skeleton of an online business, but a working system to monetize yourself and your skills.

Unfortunately, you are likely to see poor results initially. Building a business—online or offline—takes time. How do you go about growing your business and increasing the pace?

First, you need to build more visibility and increase traffic to your website. Engage actively with other relevant websites, like blogs and forums, and try to get some visibility or links to your website onto them. Engage in social media, write more blog posts, and if needed, pay for traffic using search engine or social media ads.

Second, try to get more subscribers on your email list. You do that by creating more lead magnets that entice different types of visitors to register for different types of content. For each new lead magnet you create, you also need to add related call-to-action buttons and landing pages. Make sure the new lead magnet is promoted on your website, in blog articles and mailshots, on social media, and perhaps elsewhere too.

Leverage your growing email list and send auto-scheduled emails with truly educational and valuable information regularly to nurture your audience, build trust, and keep them aware of you. As your email list grows, and as your recipients are warmed up by your high-quality educational content, you have more and more prospects who are getting prepared to pay for your skills and expertise.

Try to extend your product portfolio both horizontally and vertically. Add more product tiers in the price ladder for one topic. For example, add subscription models or a paid membership section to your website, and add more expensive product tiers that provide increasing detail or more of your personal time.

Also, try to extend your product portfolio horizontally. Your first set of vertical products most likely addressed the primary problem in your niche, for example by offering a book, a video training, a group live training, and private coaching on one topic. Are there any related problems your customers are likely to face once the primary problem is solved?

For example, if you sell web design knowledge, perhaps you can extend your product portfolio horizontally by also selling knowledge on how to set up a web shop, how to do web development, or how to do search engine optimization. If you sell knowledge on video editing, perhaps you can offer courses on producing audio podcasts or animated graphics.

This should all be consistently reiterated over time: attract more visitors, get more contacts into your email list, and have more products to sell. Repeat, repeat, repeat.

Creating a business is hard, but consistency improves the chance of success. Remember, the most difficult time is at the start. Once you are up and running, you have a working platform to extend.

Self-published eBooks

The book publishing industry has been disrupted by the self-publishing revolution. Now, practically anyone can publish a book for worldwide sales. You simply write about something you love in your favorite word-processing software, get the cover graphics designed, and upload the files for free to the large eBook web shops like Amazon, Kobo, or Apple iBooks.

You can even get a print version of your book within a couple days by using on-demand printing services like CreateSpace (a division of Amazon). Having your own non-fiction book for sale on Amazon is a major trust-builder with your audience, and works wonders as a marketing tool if you want to sell freelance work, consulting, coaching, or training.

Nothing gives you an advantage over competing consultants like giving the client a print copy of your self-published book. It establishes you as an authority and industry expert, and far more than just a consultant offering services. This may help you increase the price of your services as well.

Unfortunately, many self-published authors make little money from book sales. Is it impossible to profit from selling books?

Not necessarily. There is no contradiction in using online bookstores and building an online business platform in parallel, from which you sell higher-priced information products.

In fact, your book sales are likely to improve as you develop a thriving online platform that helps build your authority in your field. Your book sales can also be dramatically improved by promoting your books to the members of your email list harvested on your website.

You should also consider the pricing of your books and where you sell them. If you are in the low-cost camp, selling eBooks for under ten dollars on major online bookstores, you might consider an alternative. When you have an Internet platform with enough visitors, you can also sell your books on the website directly, rather than relying on a big book site to do it for you (and taking a cut of your profits).

Why would you do that?

On the big book sites, your work might not be visible in the crowd of millions of other titles, and competing books are promoted at the bottom of your sales page. That might drive customers away from your book.

Visitors to those sites often have a no-cost or low-cost mindset. With loads of competing titles available for free or selling for a couple of dollars, it becomes difficult to increase the price of your book. There is also no possibility to upsell more expensive versions of the book with bundled extras like an audio version, PhotoShop or PowerPoint design templates, checklists, or example documents.

On your website, the only book being promoted is yours. The audience is there for your authority and expertise, not a low price. If you have a respected niche website, you can easily sell a quality non-fiction book for several times the list price on Amazon. The price will not feel expensive, as there are no cheap competing books advertised beside it.

You can also sell different versions of the book with extras bundled at different price points. A $49 product can also be offered at $79 if an audio version is included, and at $99 if you offer specialized templates like legal documents that are discussed in your book. Compare that to selling the same book for under five dollars like you would on large book sites.

Of course, selling your books from your own website is only meaningful once you have a healthy traffic volume. When you've captured an eager audience, the sales will take care of themselves.

Selecting Supplies For Business

The role played by supplies is absolutely crucial to success. The more precious are the materials you use for your Business the more value your items will acquire and you can point to sell at higher price for good quality.

From it depends your customer satisfaction.

The key Points in setting your products:

·   what makes the product unique

·   the value the product brings

·   story behind the product (story why you are selling this product)

The main thing with selling your own products is that all of the responsibility is on your shoulders. You can only sell as much as you make, so you have to invest your own time into production.

The main benefit is that, aside from the cost of materials and your time, you don't have to make a significant investment up front. You also don't have to rely on suppliers. It's all on you.

How to Choose the perfect Name for your Business

Choosing a Business name can be vital to the success especially for a website since you are at the beginning I will pay particular attention to this chapter.

So before you start the first thing I recommend you to do is to do some research on the Internet.

Try to find a name that is original, standing out from the others, you will have that name for years so it is better that you are really convinced. Make sure your name can grow with your business, a name that makes sense to you but should make sense to the public as well, so envision your name before finalizing it.

Your Business name, will be also the same as for the domain of your website.

A solid keyword domain name is the key to establish a strong presence and making the resources of the Internet more reachable. With a great name, it's always easy to reach new and existing clients.

The keyword domain name is the main thing if you want to establish a strong presence and making the resources of the Internet more reachable.

Having a great name, can make it always easy to reach new and existing clients. Therefore, a number of companies are ready to spend a large amount of money to get hold of and promote a good keyword rich domain name.

In order to take advantage of search engine traffic, people choose keyword domain. By selecting a domain that is equivalent to a keyword search, websites are able to rank higher for targeted keywords and thus benefit from added traffic and more potential clients. Whether to opt for a brandable domain or a keyword domain is a choice one must make in accordance with their business plan.

Follow these simple rules to maximize the benefit of a keyword domain, accomplish success in directory submissions, and enhance site keyword density:

Structuring

Order the URL (Uniform Resource Locator) in such a manner that more vital keywords are listed before those that are less important. For example, if he target keyword is "money" then money-online.com would be more effectual than online-money.com.

Length

1. A majority of studies confirms that a number of people use two words or more in a search; as a result phrases are very useful.

2. Always stick to two-three keywords, with hyphens in between.

3. A lengthy, complex URL is more likely to be rejected by directory editors' sites from which one would like to receive links.

Correct English and Must Make Sense

1. In order to execute directory submissions and link popularity campaigns, the URL should be grammatically correct.

2. When examined by an editor, "money-online-white.com" might sound like a less-reliable resource while "white-money-online.com" sounds more justifiable and is less likely to be questioned.

Put together "power words"

In order to create a distinctive domain name that is still available, one way is to add another less important word to the mix. A few examples include: now, top, just, go to, pro, guide, online and find etc.

Avoid using most popular keyword phrases

There is intense competition for keywords in the marketplace, so stay away from the most popular keyword phrases. It is impractical to think that a new website could rank number one on a popular phrase like "Shop Online". A number of well-known companies who have been on the Internet for a few years will have the big advantage of link popularity and click popularity.

Try to register a .com domain

Always use ".com". In case it is a business website, avoid using domains ending with "ru" or "org". At once, one can consider registering a ".net" domain, but as most people are familiar with ".com", it is better to stick to convention.

In addition to the above, an understanding of the domain name system (DNS) is also vital while choosing a domain name. The DNS is set up to make regular words map to IP (Internet Protocol) addresses. In order to connect all computers on the Internet, an IP address is used by networks. A domain name can be up to sixty-three characters, comprising of letters, numbers, or the dash symbol. For example, in the world of computer networking, the web address fishing.com becomes the IP address 124.133.1.1. However, it's the domain name that people around the world use when looking for Web sites or sending an e-mail.

Finally, it is very important to choose a keyword phrase very carefully. This can be considered as one of the most critical decisions one will make regarding the success or failure of a website. One must identify the exact phrase that searchers will use to find a website. The more targeted the campaign is, the more increase in sales will be achieved.

Tip:

If you get stuck, on naming your business, don't worry. When you're first getting started you can do a DBA (doing business as) and you can change your business name anytime.

1. What is important is that you check the availability of your company name in your state with ###a href="https://brock.tv/LZM-I-5329" rel="noopener noreferrer" target="_blank">Legal Zoom.
2. Make sure your company name does not infringe on trademark

Avoiding Trademark Infringement When Choosing a Domain Name

Many webmasters erroneously believe that just because their domain name registrar says a particular domain name is 'available' that it truly is. This is not necessarily so. Even if a domain name is physically available, it may not legally be open for use. Why? It's because there might already be a company that has the rights to the keywords used within the domain name.

If this happens yet the webmaster claims the domain name anyway, they are at risk of losing it through a domain name arbitration proceeding. They could even be charged with trademark/copyright infringement if things get really ugly. For this reason it's best to make sure the keywords used in a domain name aren't protected for someone else. This article will explain how webmasters can make such a determination.

First, webmasters need to check and see if their chosen domain name resembles any existing trademark that is on the books. They will want to do this before actually investing any money in the domain name. To search existing trademarks, webmasters can visit the website of the U.S. Patent and Trademark Office which is USPTO.gov. From here they can search a database that contains current trademarks as well as those that are pending.

If a domain name is similar to a registered or pending trademark, webmasters need to evaluate whether the domain name is still worth taking. Usually, if a site is not selling the same types of merchandise or services that the other business is selling and the trademark is not popular, a webmaster probably won't get into legal trouble if they decide to go on and register the domain name. To be completely sure, webmasters can run the domain name by a trademark attorney. It shouldn't cost too much for an hour consultation.

Of course, if a webmaster would prefer zero percent risk, they can simply try to think of another domain name. When they go about doing this, they need to be more generic and less creative in what they come up with. Using search engine keywords for a domain name is one such strategy. Webmasters can also look into using dictionary terms. If all else fails they can take a generic term and combine it with a term that is less likely to be taken, such as their first and last name.

Either way, once a suitable domain name has been chosen, webmasters should consider getting it trademarked themselves, especially if they are using it to help brand their business. With an official trademark, a webmaster has more legal power should another company try to take them to court. And since there's no shortage of domain name bullies, (companies that try to steal profitable domain names from smaller enterprises), a webmaster should use all legal avenues available to protect the rights of their business.

In conclusion, by checking whether or not a domain name has keywords that are part of a trademark, webmasters lessen the risk that they will have legal problems in the future. If there are problems, and a domain name arbitration proceeding does not rule in a webmaster's favor, they can turn to The Domain Name Rights Coalition.

What tools can I use to get start building my online business?

Knowing where to start may be a big problem for people without knowledge on web design and Internet marketing. In this section, I will cover the most important tools you can use to build an online presence, improve your authority, perform Internet marketing, and build an online business.

The website is the basis for any online business. In the early years, a website was designed by coding HTML tags in a pure text editor, and those files would then be uploaded to the webserver using an FTP transfer tool.

That was cumbersome and required the user to know how to write computer code. Nowadays virtually all websites are built using content management systems (CMS) that are very easy to use and can be operated by anyone. Content management systems include a web-based configuration and administration panel where you can create menus, pages, blog articles, and more, which are then published to the website automatically.

The most popular content management systems are Joomla and WordPress, both of which are free open-source options that can be installed on your own servers. However, by far the best solution is to rent web space from a company that can host a Joomla or WordPress installation for you. There are many web hosting services available, for example SiteGround and HostGator, that charge a low fee per month, and provide email accounts and other tools at the same time.

Nowadays WordPress is the most popular choice, thanks to its ease-of-use and drag-and-drop design capabilities. Arguably, Joomla is somewhat faster, but it is more cumbersome to work with.

Market Your Business Online

To adjust the look and feel of your website, install a free or paid theme into your Joomla or WordPress site. This changes the personality of your website and should be aligned with your branding. There are tens of thousands of Joomla and WordPress themes available, for example from ThemeForest.

No website owners should ignore installing Google Analytics, which is a free cloud service that helps track exactly how your website visitors behave when they visit your site. Accounts are free and only require that you install a small tracking code on your website. You can then enjoy detailed statistics on exactly how your website performs and what your visitors are doing.

For general office tasks, you will need tools like an email client, a word processor, presentation software, and a spreadsheet program. There are four main options:

· Microsoft Office 365 with Word, Excel, PowerPoint and Outlook for email and calendars. After a late start, Microsoft now offers excellent versions of the Office package for Mac computers and the iPhone, iPad, and even the Apple Watch. Office 365 is now offered for a low-cost monthly fee.

·   For a completely free solution, use OpenOffice, which is free and open-source. It is available for Apple OS X, Microsoft Windows, and Linux systems.

·   If you are in the Apple camp, you can use the Pages word processor, Numbers spreadsheet program, and Keynotes presentation software for free.

·   For a completely cloud-based solution, Google Apps is a good choice.

If you want a centralized repository for your notes and other records, Evernote or Microsoft OneNote are both great choices. Both have cross-platform support such that you can access your notes and records from any device, and they are all synchronized from a cloud server.

For cloud-based file storage, you can use DropBox, Microsoft OneDrive, Apple's iCloud Drive, or Amazon's S3 cloud hosting. They all provide cheap file storage solutions, with backup, that can be accessed from any device or platform.

Skype has a natural place in your toolbox. Not only does it allow you to call for free to anyone in the world (Skype-to-Skype) using your computer and the Internet, but it also provides the possibility to setup a group call for free. Skype also supports video calls and video conferencing, as well as screen sharing and file transfer. The ability to transfer files is an unexpected strength of Skype. It solves the problem of emailing oversized files, as Skype happily transfers a 1GB file without problem.

Skype also provides some paid services; like the possibility to call out to the normal land line system in any country, such that you do not pay for the international call but only for the connection out to the local number from their server in that country.

Skype also offers local phone numbers that allow customers to call in to a normal land line phone number, which is redirected to your Skype account on your computer. That way, you can easily set up one or more local phone numbers in any country, which are redirected to your laptop no matter where you are. Additionally, Skype offers voice mail and some other services.

Facetime is Apple's answer to Skype, but it is limited and only works on Apple products, which severely limits its use.

With the eCamm extension for Skype or Facetime, you can record voice or video calls and save them for later editing and publication, perhaps as recorded podcast interviews or video trainings.

Grasshopper is another powerful virtual phone system. In addition to many of the phone functions of Skype, it supports toll-free numbers, voice menus to different departments, sending voicemails or fax to your email account, and more. It is a great solution for distributed or remote teams.

An excellent solution for web meetings with screen sharing and screen recording features is GotoMeeting from Citrix, which also works for webinars with a limited set of participants. With GotoMeeting, you can even give the controls (your mouse and keyboard) to a remote attendee, or you can take over a remote computer, which is excellent for remote support, troubleshooting, or work on someone else's computer.

Market Your Business Online

Managing all your social media channels can be very time consuming, but there are tools to help. To publish a message on many social media channels automatically, monitor social media channels, schedule queued messages, or otherwise manage social media channels, check out Feedly, Buffer, HootSuite, SocialOomph, SocialBro, SproutSocial, Tweeapi, or Edgar.

For more advanced photo editing, you can use the free GIMP or the industry-standard but expensive Adobe Photoshop. For simple photo editing, you can use Apple iPhoto or Microsoft Paint.

You can record movies using a digital camera or even your smartphone, and edit them using Apple iMovie or Microsoft Movie Maker. For more professional solutions, look at Apple's Final Cut or Adobe Premier.

To record your screen when you run a PowerPoint presentation or demo software, you can use Camtasia on Windows or Apple Quicktime or Screenflow on Mac. Alternatively, use Skype with a screen recorder add-on.

There are many options for recording and editing audio. A free but somewhat complicated solution is Audacity, or you can use GarageBand on Apple platforms. You can also use the Adobe Audition software, or Auphonic sound editing cloud-service.

If you want to prepare the text you are reading in advance and read it smoothly while recording, you can use the free dvPrompter iPad app. It allows you to read the auto-scrolling text so you remember what to say when you talk into the camera or microphone.

For production of animated illustrations or banner ads, you can try the free Google Web Designer tool.

A podcast is a series of audio files that is distributed as a channel your audience can subscribe to. A podcast must be published in a special format that podcast reader software can understand, and is thus different from just publishing a series of MP3 audio files on your website.

If you produce audio podcasts, the easiest thing is to host them on a cloud service such as SoundCloud or LibSyn. You can also register your podcast with Apple's iTunes to make your podcasts visible to Apple users and the podcast app on the iPhone.

Video tutorials and other video movies can be published on YouTube or Vimeo. High-end solutions include Wistia and VidYard.

A webinar is a meeting or presentation with remote attendees that join through their computers over the Internet. You can share your screen and record sound. The remote attendees can see your screen on their computer and hear your live audio.

Webinars are thus perfect for product presentations, trainings, or remote coaching. A great webinar solution for small webinars is GotoMeeting from Citrix, while their GotoWebinar service is an excellent solution supporting hundreds of concurrent attendees. GotoWebinar includes services like registration and attendee management, scheduling of webinar series, in-webinar poll questions, and post-webinar surveys.

Market Your Business Online

Using a marketing automation system, you can create an automated workflow through which you send a series of emails automatically to the website visitors who register in a form. In its simplest form, this is just email marketing or auto-responders dropping emails to leads in your database. Sending a series of emails automatically is also known as drip emailing.

Easy to use examples include AWeber, MailChimp, GetResponse, or LeadPages. Middle-end solutions include Infusion or Leadsius. High-end systems that can do some advanced tricks are, for example, HubSpot, Marketo, and SalesForce Pardot. These go well beyond basic functionalities, and are prohibitively expensive for small businesses.

If you have a business with a reasonable amount of real customers already, a customer support portal like ZenDesk can bring structure and better service to your customer queries. With ZenDesk or similar customer service systems, you can track incoming sales or support requests, offer self-service portals, and more.

Writing good text, also known as copywriting, is not as easy as it may seem. Admittedly, most word processors have a built in spelling and grammar checker. If you want something a lot better, use Grammarly, which is about the best grammar checker around. Their product is available both as Windows and Mac software, as well as a cloud service.

In case you want to charge for digital content or services on your website, you need a payment solution. Several options exist.

PayPal may be the easiest solution, through which your customers can send money to you using only your email address, provided both of you have a PayPal account connected to your bank account. You can also embed BuyNow or AddToCart buttons on your website, manage subscription payments, and more.

Other solutions include e-Junkie, SendOwl, and Gumroad, which are focused on selling digital files on the Internet. Stripe is another solution that is easy to use and has deeper integration with your website. Stripe requires some programming on the website to integrate it, although it is relatively easy.

Membership site solutions and online video training platforms (like Teachable) often include payment solutions too.

Sometimes you may need to use freelancers to help with particular tasks or skills, such as web design, graphics design, copywriting, or book editing. You can find freelancers at all price points on websites like Upwork, Freelancer, Fiverr, or 99designs.

E- commerce Store – Build your own

If you have a product oriented business, the Internet offers a unique ability to reach a broad audience. With new technology, it is easy to build your own e-commerce store.

E-commerce Store

Today's world is an E-commerce (electronic commerce or e-com) world. E-commerce, clearly termed as web commerce, basically means selling of merchandise or services over the Internet with electronic transactions and also through a secure network. E-com is not merely buying and selling or providing services but it is also a method of advertising and marketing through an electronic system as well. E-com also means facilitating the progress of commercial transactions electronically. Right now e-com is a well-established technology in all major countries. In most cases Internet marketing requires you to have your own E-commerce store for maximum return.

<u>Requirements of an E-commerce Store</u>

Building an e-commerce store is not an easy job. Software is required that can manage customers as well as their needs. E-commerce software should be able to handle inventory, shipping and handling costs, taxes, dispatching and payment processing of client's orders. You may encounter many options when setting out to build an e commerce store. Before choosing any of them it is important to have a clear view of your requirements. Technical requirements might include coupons, tracking systems, customer login options or any number of other things. Other requirements include what type of impression you want to provide to your valuable clients.

Study the Sales and Marketing Cycle to Determine Your Needs

Before you opt for any of solutions for building e commerce store, study the basic model of e commerce that represents the entire sales and marketing cycle. The first building block of this cycle is audience in which you define what type of customers you will target. Second are commodities, in which you characterize the types of products you will put on the market. Third is customer support where you will answer the questions and offer solutions to clients' or potential clients' problems. Next are advertising, marketing and endorsement where a business promotes the products or services. Then there is transaction processing, the most important technical phase of the cycle, which will handle orders, taxes, payment processing and order delivery.

Transactions may be automatic or manual. In manual processing you have to enter credit card information manually through an offline terminal. In the case of automatic processing a client's order form will be setup with a program that processes and charges the credit card for you. After that there are post-deal services regarding how you provide solutions and services after the sale. Last but not least is brand name with which you will create a distinctive business image to correspond with customers. Nobody is going to pay attention to your online store unless something catches their eye.

Refund Policy

Obviously I'd leave about the refund policy, privacy policy, terms of service and we will get onto in fact what you do. Just click generate,

It's up to you what your refund policy is and I for example go the 28 days.

You can make all the points clear, by going to Settings and then check-out, and then scroll down to 'Refund, Privacy, TOS statements'. On the right side you will find the tab 'Generate Sample Refund Policy', click on it and it will generate a Policy automatically that you can customized at your preference.

Or, by using one of online policy generators like www.termly.io, which helps you to create the document step by step. Bear in mind this is all initial stuff, perfect for starting, and that you will need to speak with a consultant or accountant.

Once you are happy with that, just copy it and paste it in your dedicate page.

Let's have a look here the conditions, you should include:

The period of time you send the money back,

What countries are eligible for refunds and returns,

The period of time when customers are eligible for a return,

Items that cannot be returned,

Variants of what they may get: refund only, return and refund, store credit only, exchange only — or some of them, or all of them,

Who pays for shipping, your store or a client,

Market Your Business Online

Your contacts for returns and address the package should be sanded back.

Online Store: the unmissable pages

Then you go filling all the other pages. Add essential pages of your store:

- About us

- FAQs

- Contact us

- Order Tracking

- Shipping and Delivery

- Return Policy

- Privacy Policy

- Terms of Service

Go to Settings and then check-out, and then scroll down to 'Refund, Privacy, TOS statements'. On the right side you will find the tab 'Generate Sample Refund Policy', click on it and it will generate a Policy automatically that you can customized at your preference.

Tips: Loads of people do apply different shipping model. Obviously you can apply whatever you like, but if I can give you a little tip that brought some little more of the flavor of success, Instead of setting the free plus shipping model that a lot of people follow. I would rather offer a standard free shipping on all of my orders. It is easier, avoid confusion and so less headaches.

All you do is put type in, don't type in standard shipping, type of free shipping. Customers will see this at checkout and wherever you can write free shipping. It is a huge factor in your conversion rates and making people buy on your store. If you don't have free shipping, less people are going to make purchases on your store.

How To Expand Your Business Once Started

If you are always working hard, and if you have the right strategies to help grow your business, then after some time you will see that your business is growing.

If you stop working when things are slow, then it will be really difficult to achieve success with your business.

It is hard to see the beginning of any activity. You must be patient and work without seeing any results for a long time. But when you finally see the results, keep working on them so they can increase even more!

The beginning is the most difficult part as in any type of activity, you will have to be patient and work without seeing any kind of result, committing yourself with the sole aim of being able to see them grow one step at a time.

When you finally see the results coming, you absolutely won't have to stop, but focus on those processes that will allow you to increase them further.

Improving customer experience

It is possible to greatly improve the browsing and purchasing experience of your customers in your store.

The ease of browsing your site will entice your users to come back.

Make sure you make the site fast (Siteground in this for our experience has proved to be the best for now), make payments easy to make, and don't forget to always enter payment terms, shipping terms, return conditions.

It is very important to be extremely honest about shipping times, they must be absolutely aware of the time needed to receive the product purchased.

It is not a big problem for people to wait as long as they are aware that it will still be necessary to do so.

Product catalog update

Always remember to keep offered.

It always analyzes the sales data of the articles, to understand if the products marketed are actually of customer satisfaction or if maybe it may be necessary to study a reorganization of their catalog.

Opening new stores

Market Your Business Online

The launch of the first store always represents an opportunity to study the market and acquire those skills that will allow you to really make the strategies to achieve success with your business.

Once you have digested this knowledge, why not consider the idea of launching new stores?

You will realize with the successive launches of the enormous quantity of skills acquired with the first store, knowledge that will allow you to achieve the desired results much more easily and quickly.

Explore

There is so much to learn, I can always guarantee it.

For this reason, once you have acquired your personal experience, you will be able to build new strategies based on your specific business history and maybe you can share new winning strategies with the community to achieve success with.

Being Digital Entrepreneurs also means this, so much and so much research, testing, development and analysis of results.

We have finished our journey based on operational steps to achieve success.

We hope this guide of ours can help you on your journey, failures on failures have resulted us, but today we can share all that we have learned from our failures hoping that you will appreciate our efforts.

Final words

This book has given you the tools to take the next step. With these tools, you can go from being someone who knows and is skilled at something, to someone who is an expert with authority. You will have a marketing platform that will be your own online business.

You can use this book to build a list of people who are interested in what you have to say. You can then send them information and sell your knowledge as digital products.

Good luck!

Printed by Libri Plureos GmbH in Hamburg,
Germany